DRAW 50 HORSES

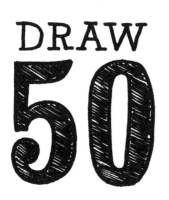

*The Step-by-Step Way to Draw Broncos,
Arabians, Thoroughbreds, Dancers, Prancers,
and Many More . . .*

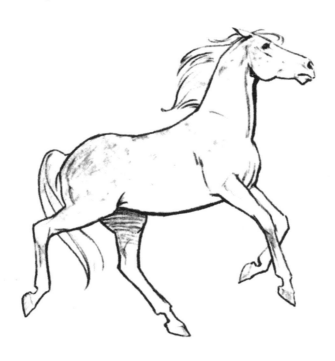

LEE J. AMES

Watson-Guptill Publications, New York

WATSON-GUPTILL and the WG and Horse designs are
registered trademarks of Random House, Inc.

Originally published in hardcover in the United States by
Doubleday, a division of Random House Inc., New York, in 1984.

Library of Congress Cataloging-in-Publication Data

Ames, Lee J.
    Draw 50 horses / Lee J. Ames

    p. cm.
1. Horses in art—Juvenile literature. 2. Drawing—Technique—Juvenile literature. [1. Horses in art. 2. Animal painting and illustration. 3. Drawing—Technique]. I. Title. II. Title: Draw fifty horses.

NC783.8.H65 A43 1984
743/.69725

                    81043646

ISBN 978-0-8230-8581-1
eISBN 978-0-307-79502-1

Printed in the United States of America

10 9 8 7 6 5 4 3 2 1

BOOKS IN THIS SERIES

- *Draw 50 Airplanes, Aircraft, and Spacecraft*
- *Draw 50 Aliens*
- *Draw 50 Animal 'Toons*
- *Draw 50 Animals*
- *Draw 50 Athletes*
- *Draw 50 Baby Animals*
- *Draw 50 Beasties*
- *Draw 50 Birds*
- *Draw 50 Boats, Ships, Trucks, and Trains*
- *Draw 50 Buildings and Other Structures*
- *Draw 50 Cars, Trucks, and Motorcycles*
- *Draw 50 Cats*
- *Draw 50 Creepy Crawlies*
- *Draw 50 Dinosaurs and Other Prehistoric Animals*
- *Draw 50 Dogs*
- *Draw 50 Endangered Animals*
- *Draw 50 Famous Cartoons*
- *Draw 50 Flowers, Trees, and Other Plants*
- *Draw 50 Horses*
- *Draw 50 Magical Creatures*
- *Draw 50 Monsters*
- *Draw 50 People*
- *Draw 50 Princesses*
- *Draw 50 Sharks, Whales, and Other Sea Creatures*
- *Draw 50 Vehicles*
- *Draw the Draw 50 Way*

DRAW 50 HORSES

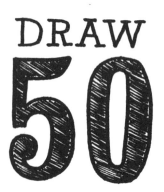

The Step-by-Step Way to Draw Broncos,
Arabians, Thoroughbreds, Dancers, Prancers,
and Many More . . .

To Alison, regal and elegant . . .

. . . and thank you, Tamara Scott, for your help.

To the Reader

Broncos, Arabians, thoroughbreds, dancers and prancers —here they all are. By following simple, step-by-step instructions, you can draw them.

Start by gathering your equipment. You will need paper, medium and/or soft pencils, and a kneaded eraser (available at art supply stores). You might also wish to use India ink, a fine brush or pen, or perhaps a fine pointed felt-tip or ball-point pen.

Next, choose one of the horses...you needn't start with the first illustration. As you begin, remember that the first few steps—the foundation of the drawing—are the most important. If they are not right, the end result will be distorted. So, follow these steps *very carefully* and keep your lines *very* light. In order that they can be clearly seen, these steps are shown darker in this book than you should draw them. You can lighten your lines by gently pressing them with the kneaded eraser.

Make sure step one is accurate before you go on to step two. To check your own accuracy, hold the work up to a mirror after a few steps. By reversing the image, the mirror gives you a new view of the drawing. If you haven't done it quite right, you may notice that your drawing is out of proportion or off to one side.

You can reinforce the drawing by going over the completed final step with India ink and a fine brush or pen; or with the felt-tip or ball-point. When the ink has dried thoroughly, gently remove the pencil lines with the kneaded eraser.

Don't get discouraged if, at first, you find it difficult to duplicate the shapes pictured. Just keep at it, and in no time you'll be able to make the pencil go just where you wish. Drawing, like any other skill, requires patience, practice, and perseverance.

Remember, this book presents only one method of drawing. In a most enjoyable way, it will help you develop a certain skill and control. But there are many other ways of drawing to which you can apply this skill, and the more of them you explore, the more interesting your drawings will be.

Lee J. Ames

To the Parent or Teacher

Drawing, like any other skill, requires practice and discipline. But this does not mean that rewards cannot be found along every step of the way.

While contemporary methods of art instruction rightly emphasize freedom of expression and experimentation, they often lose sight of a very basic, traditional and valuable approach: the "follow me, step by step" way that I learned as a youth.

Just as a beginning musician is given simple, beautiful melodies to play, so too the young artist needs to gain a sense of satisfaction and pride in his/her work as soon as possible. The "do as I do" steps that I have laid out here provide the opportunity to mimic finished images, pictures the young artist is eager to draw.

Mimicry is prerequisite for developing creativity. We learn the use of our tools through mimicry, and once we have those tools we are free to express ourselves in whatever fashion we choose. The use of this book will help lay a solid foundation for the child, one that can be continued with other books in the Draw 50 series, or even used to complement different approaches to drawing.

Above all, the joy of making a credible, attractive image will encourage the child to continue and grow as an artist, giving him even more of a sense of pride and accomplishment when his friends say, "Peter can draw a horse better than anyone else!"

Lee J. Ames

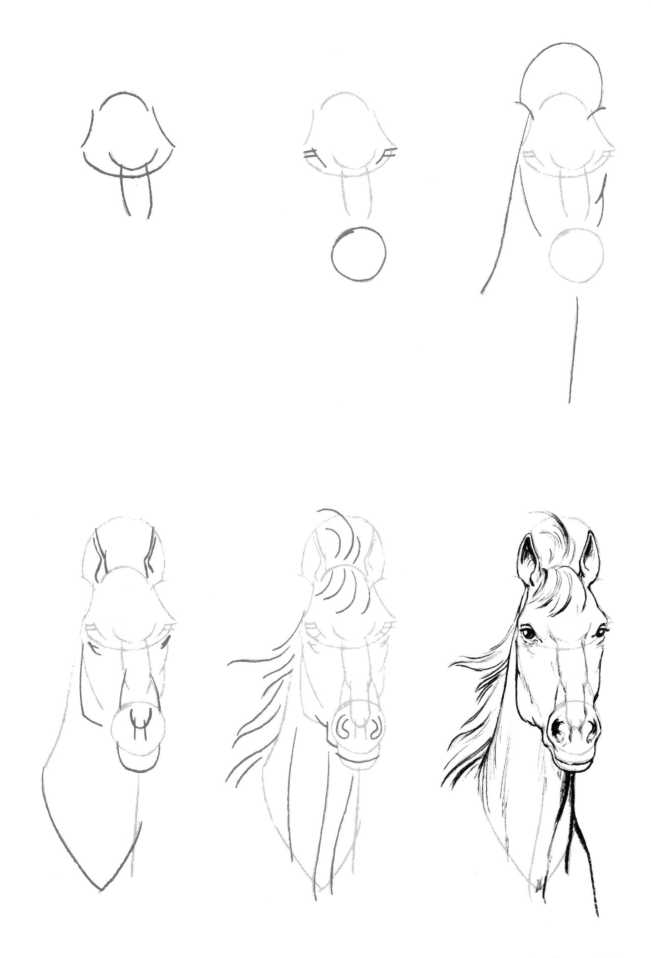

Portrait, frontal view

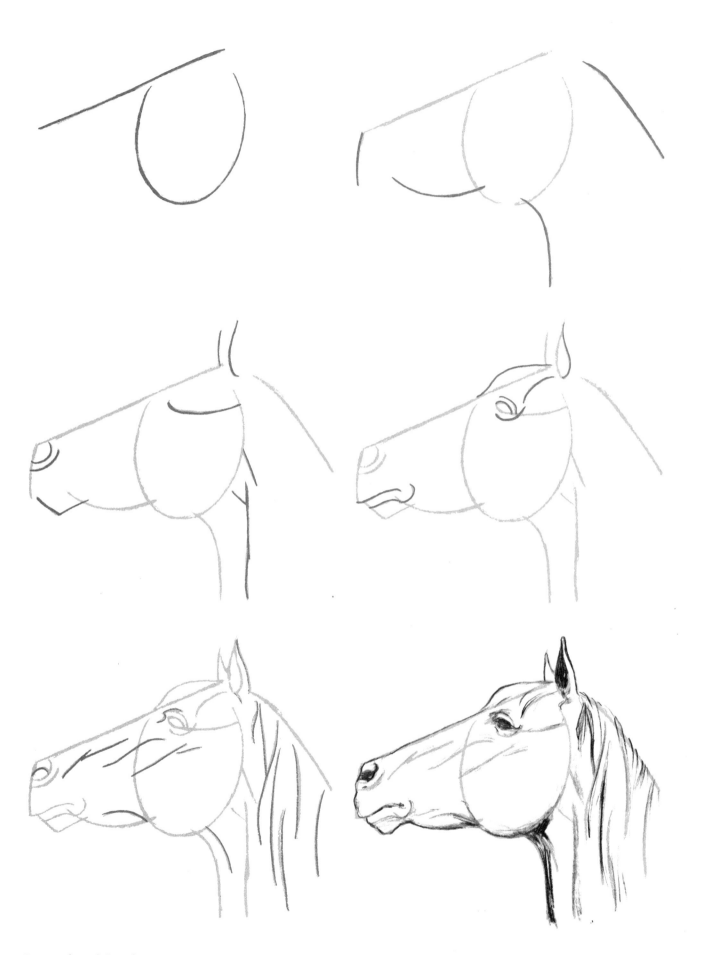

Portrait, side view

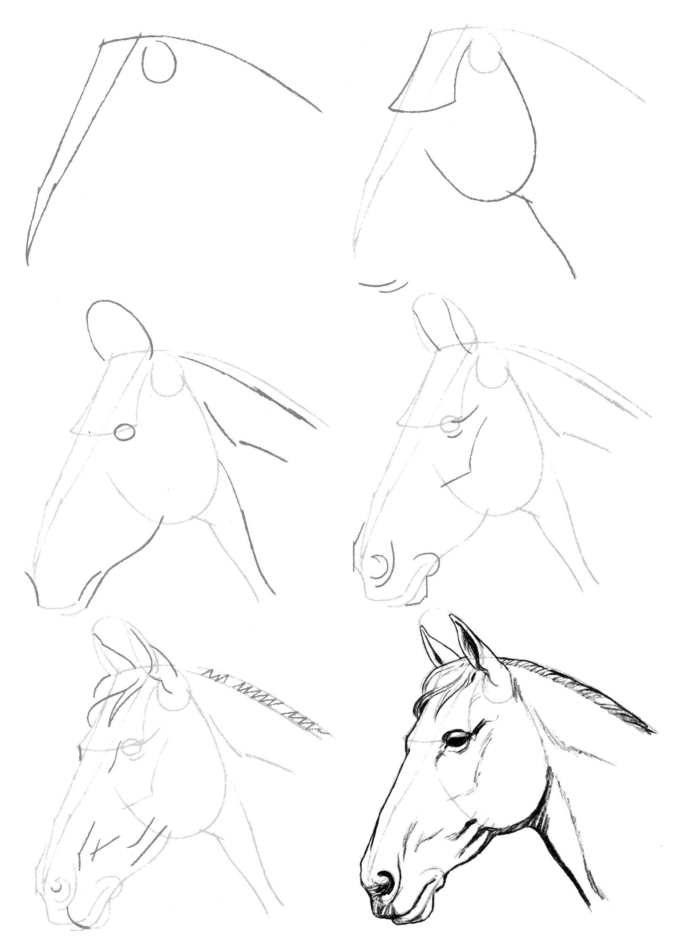

Portrait, side view

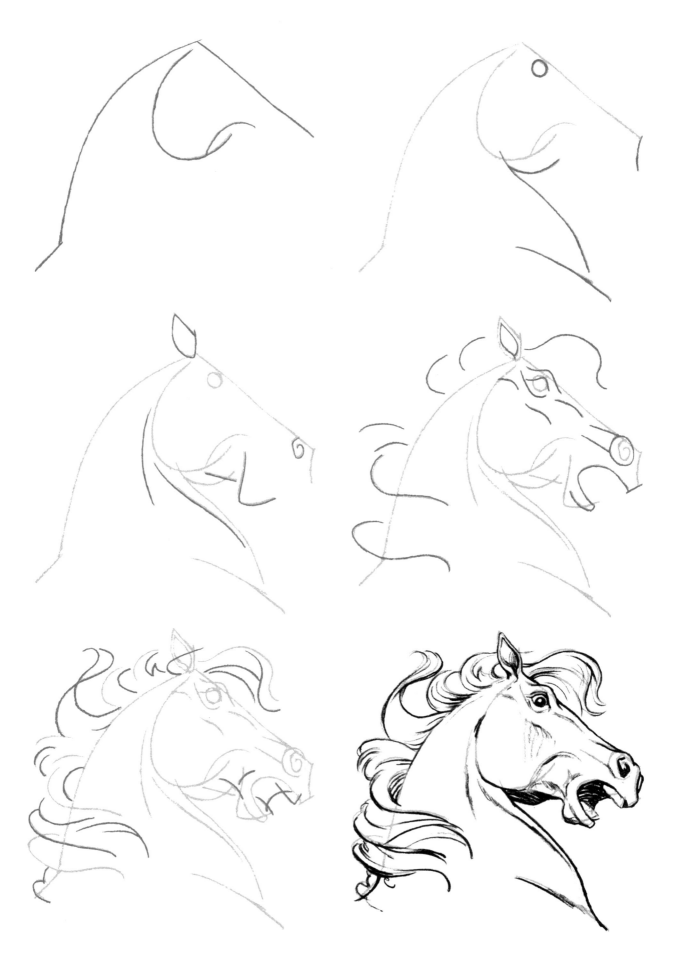

Portrait, rearing

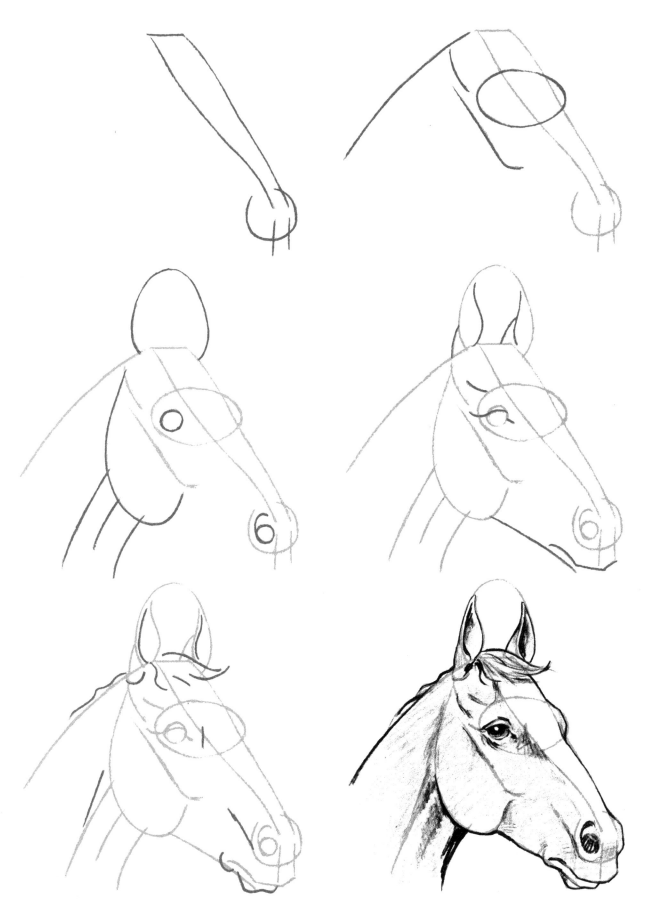

Portrait, blaze

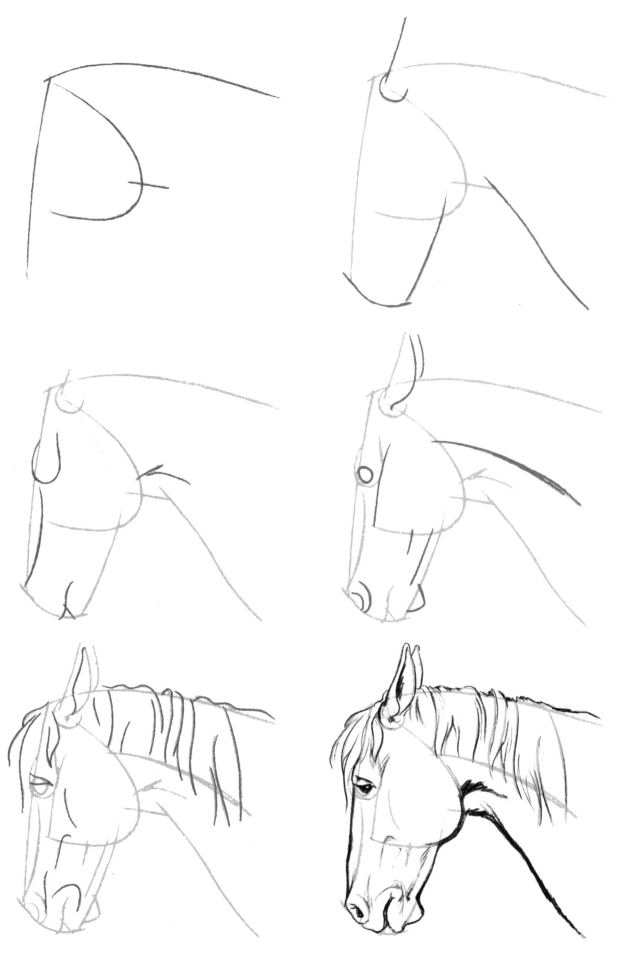

Portrait, nag

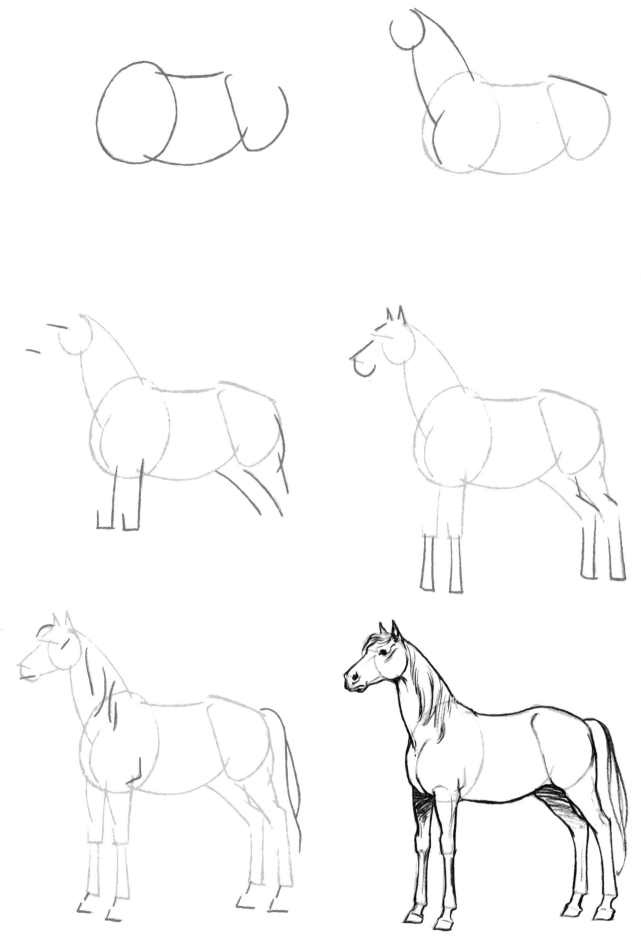

Arabian

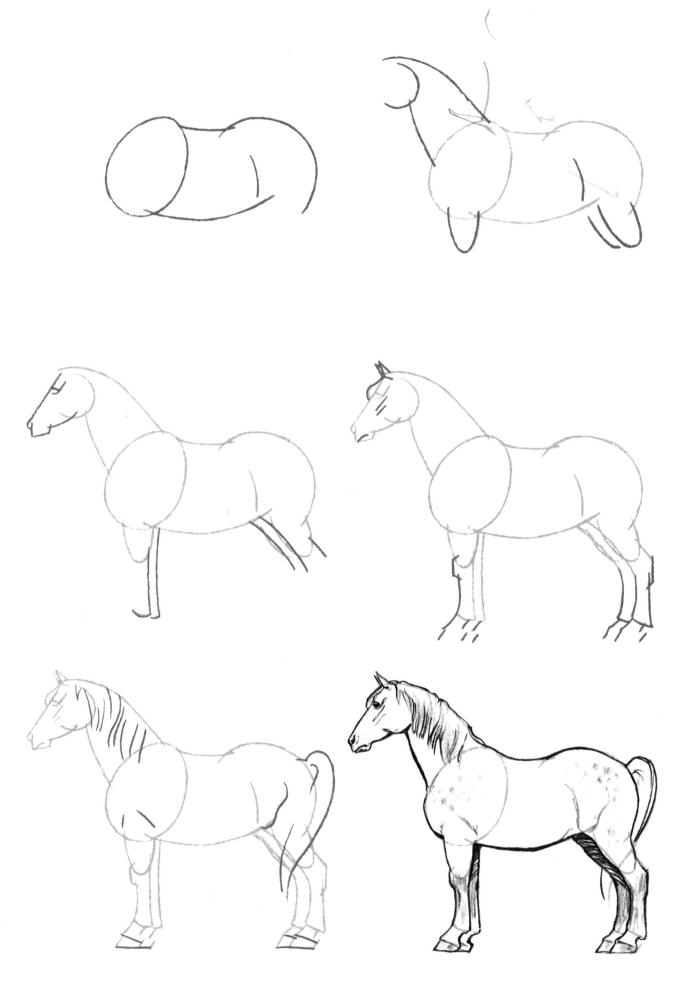

Percheron

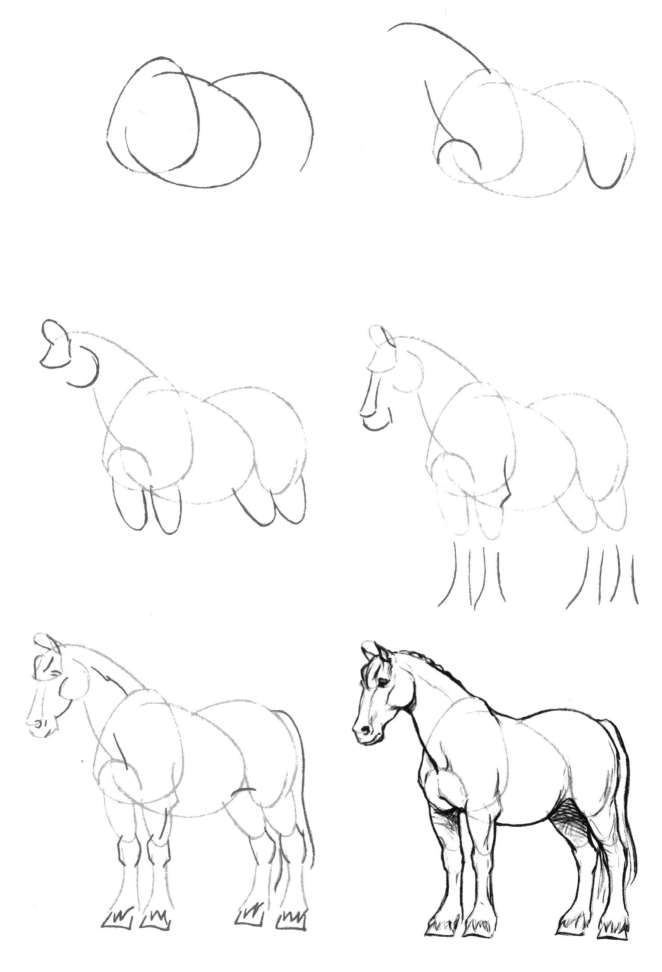

Clydesdale

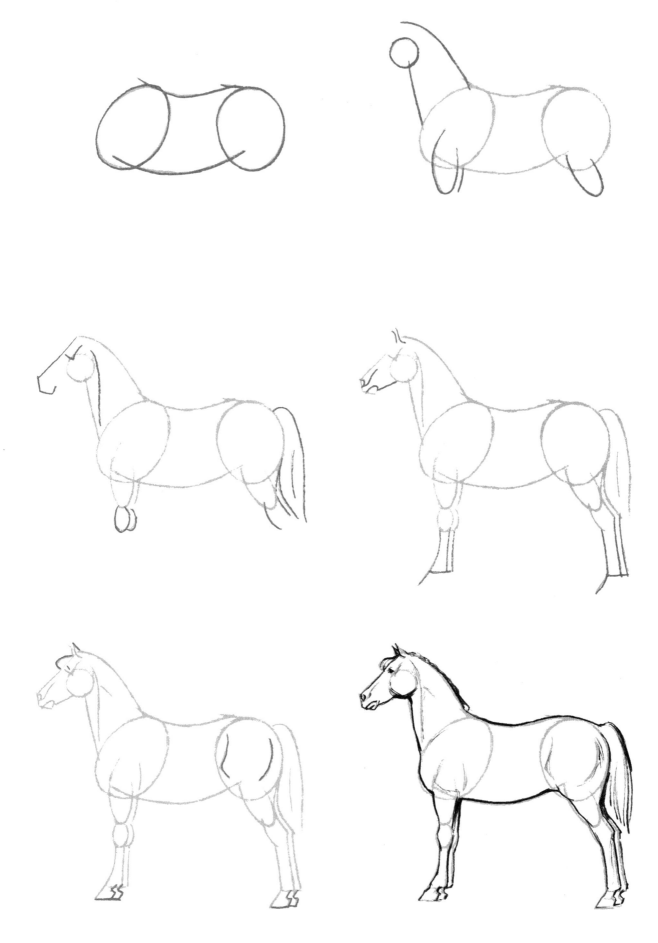

Morgan

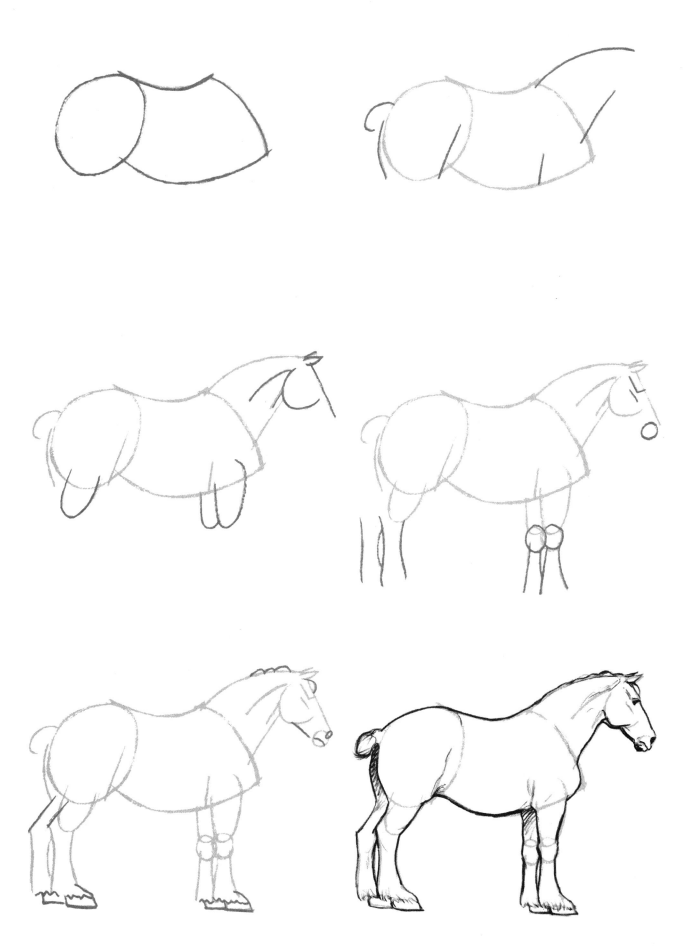

Shire

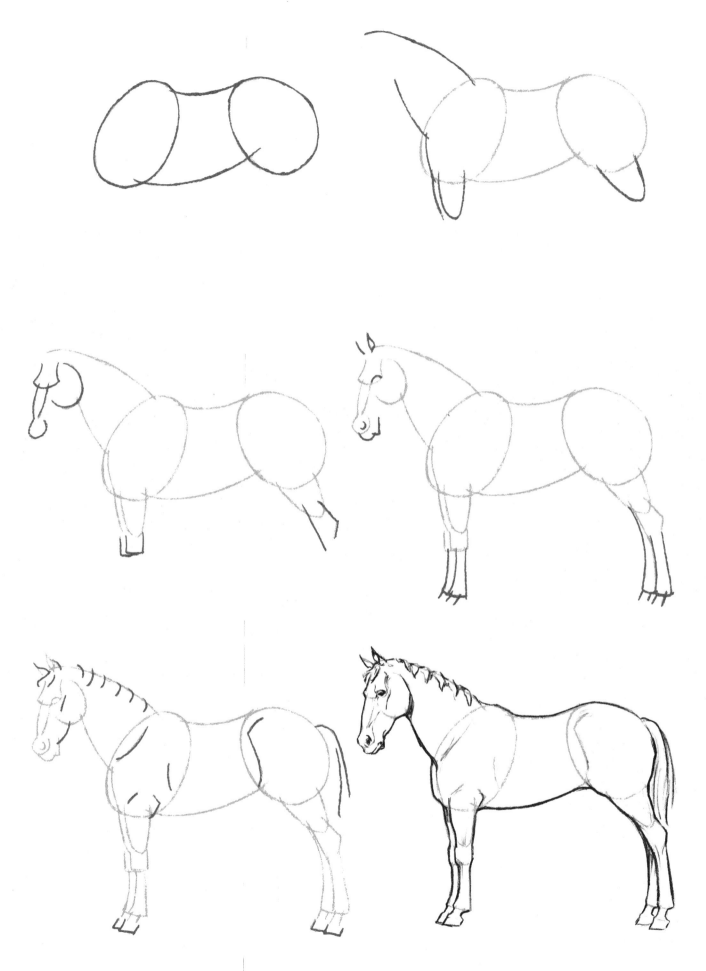

Tennessee Walking Horse

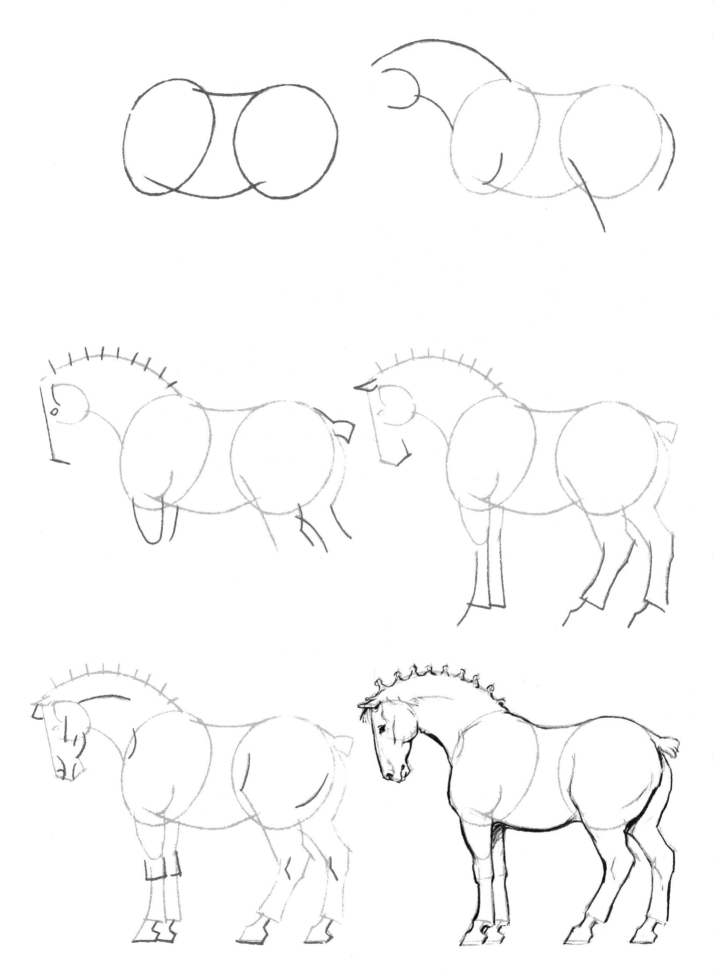

Belgian

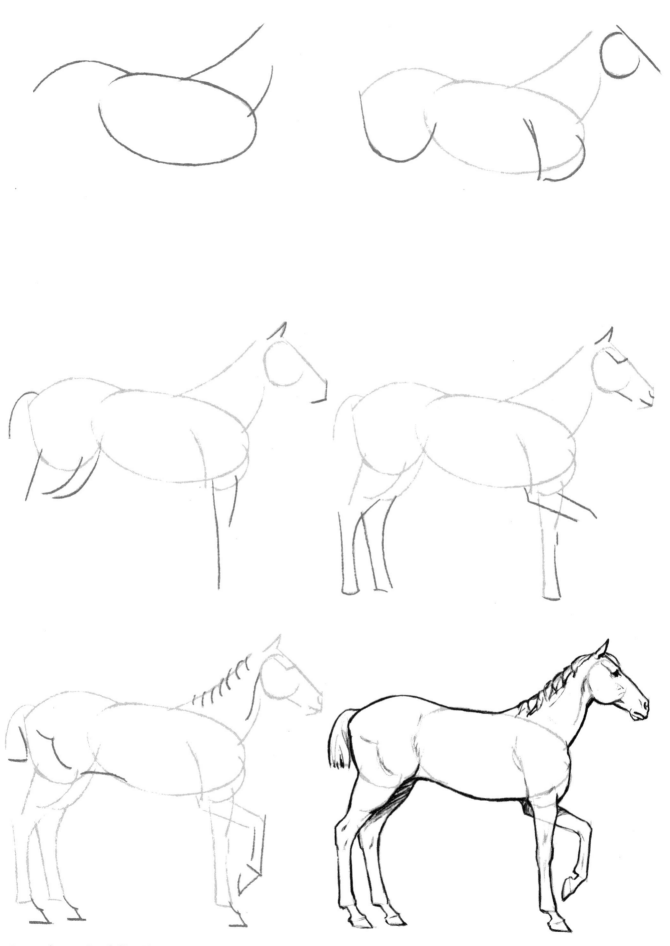

American Saddle Horse

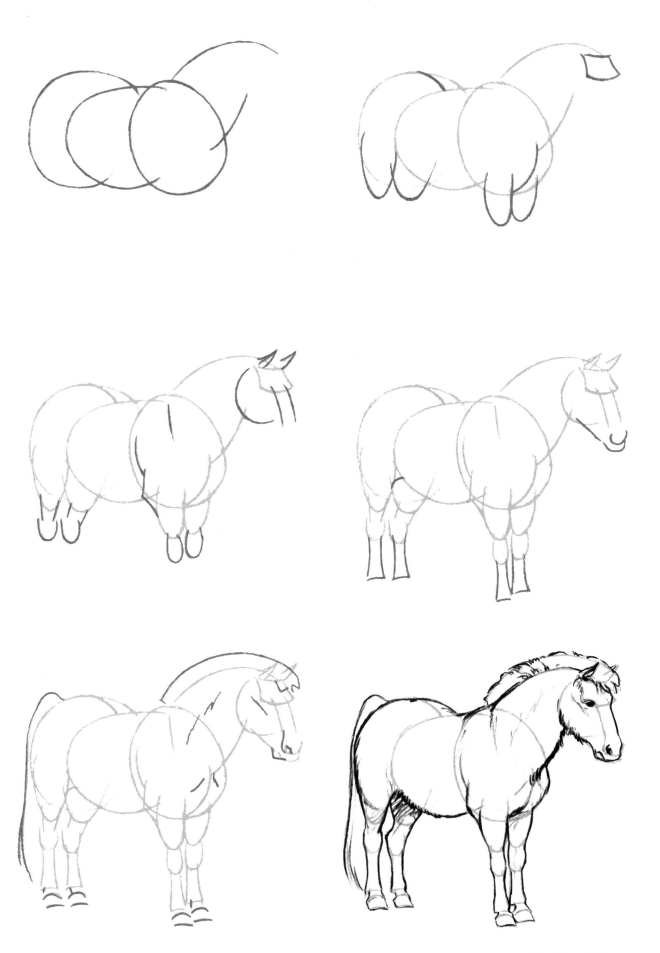

Shetland Pony

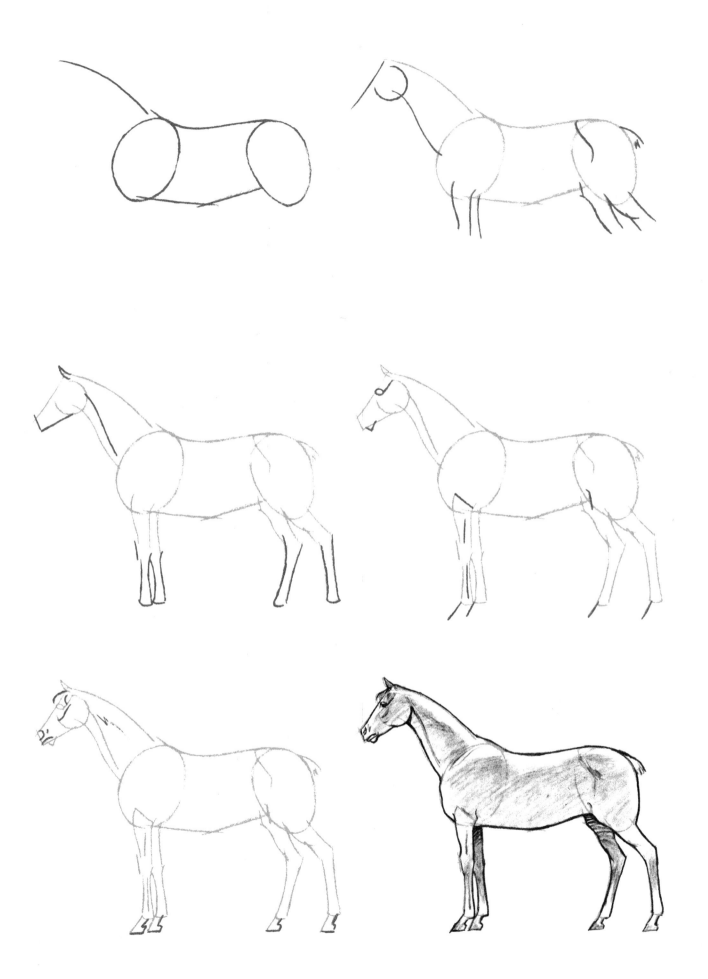

Thoroughbred

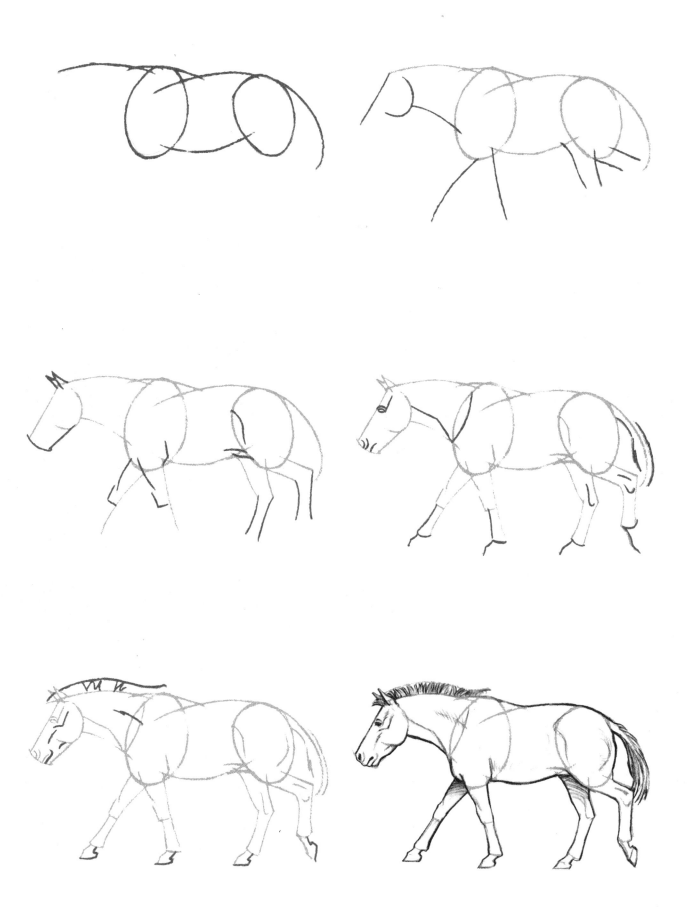

Przhevalski (wild Asian horse)

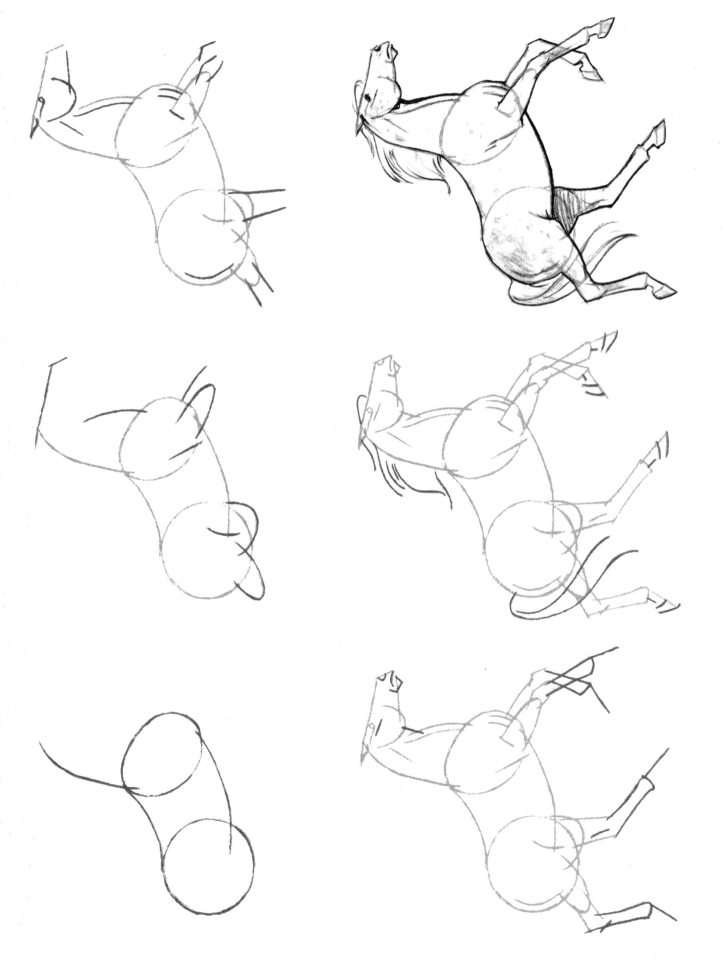

Appaloosa

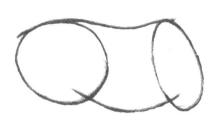
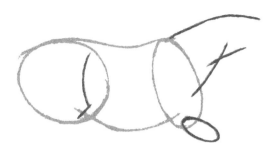
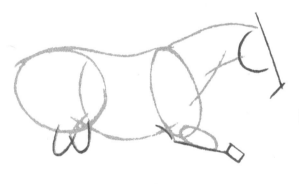
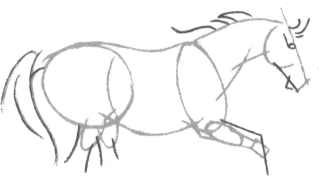
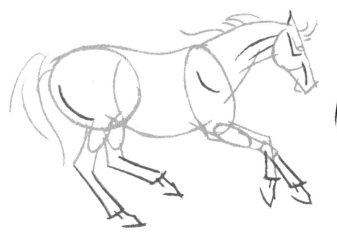
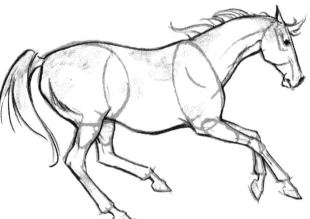

Pinto

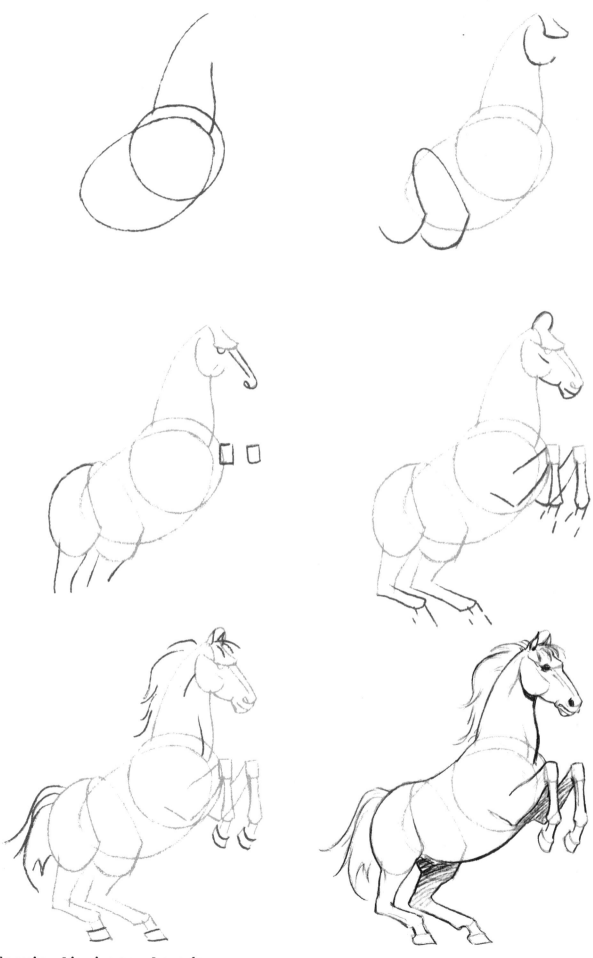

Performing Lippizaner, Levade

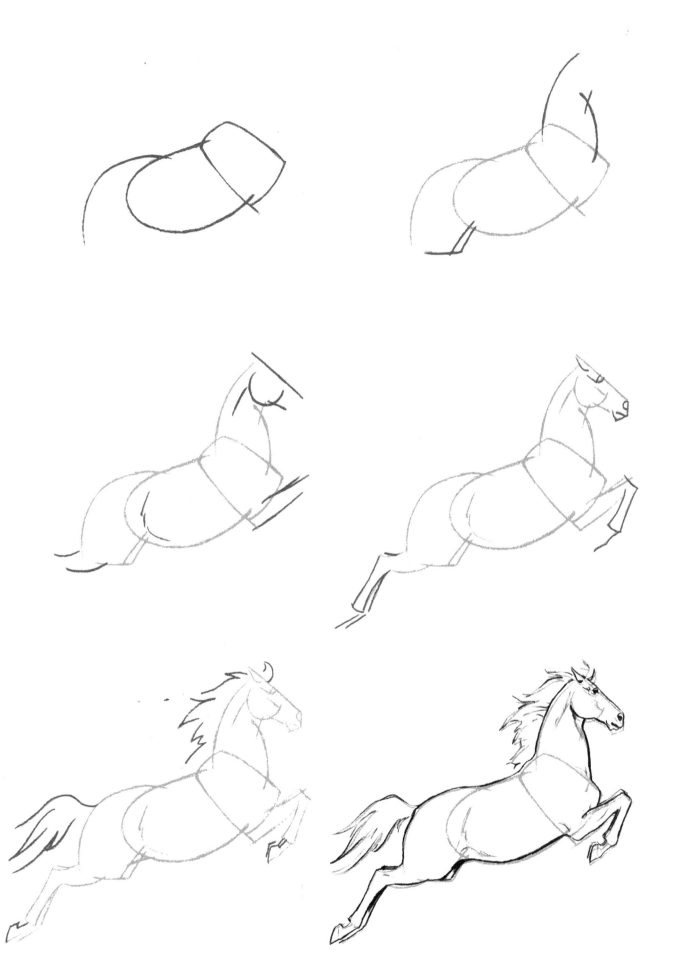

Performing Lippizaner, Capriole

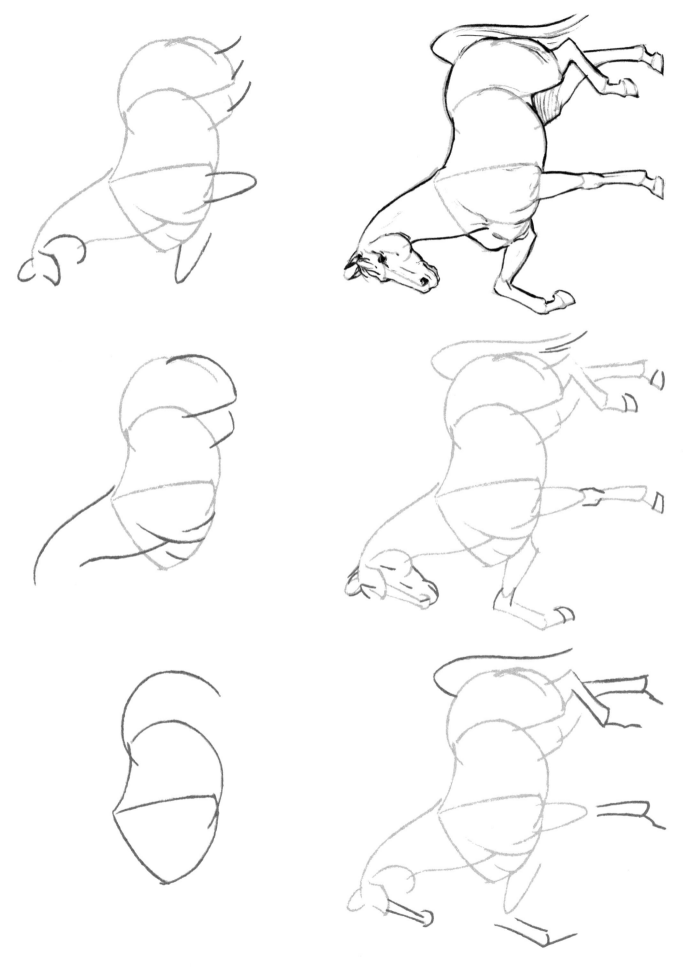

Performing Lippizaner, Piaffe

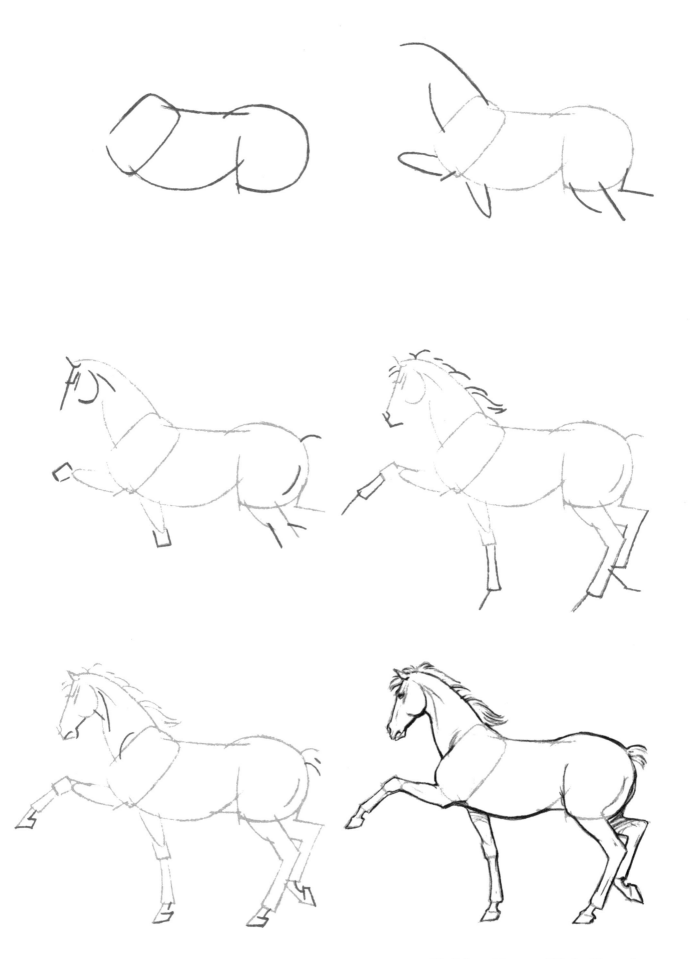

Tennessee Walking Horse, High-Stepping

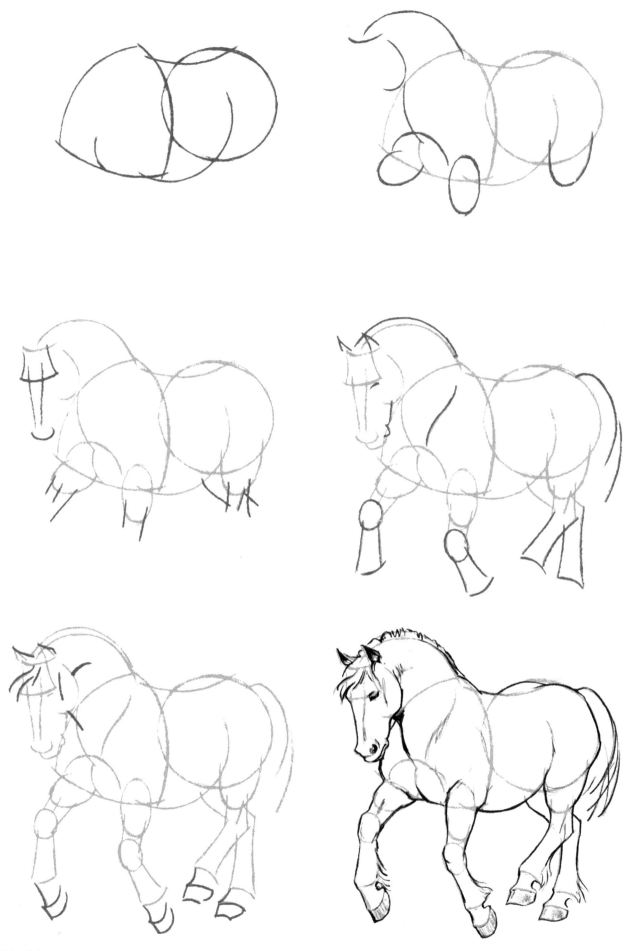

Workhorse

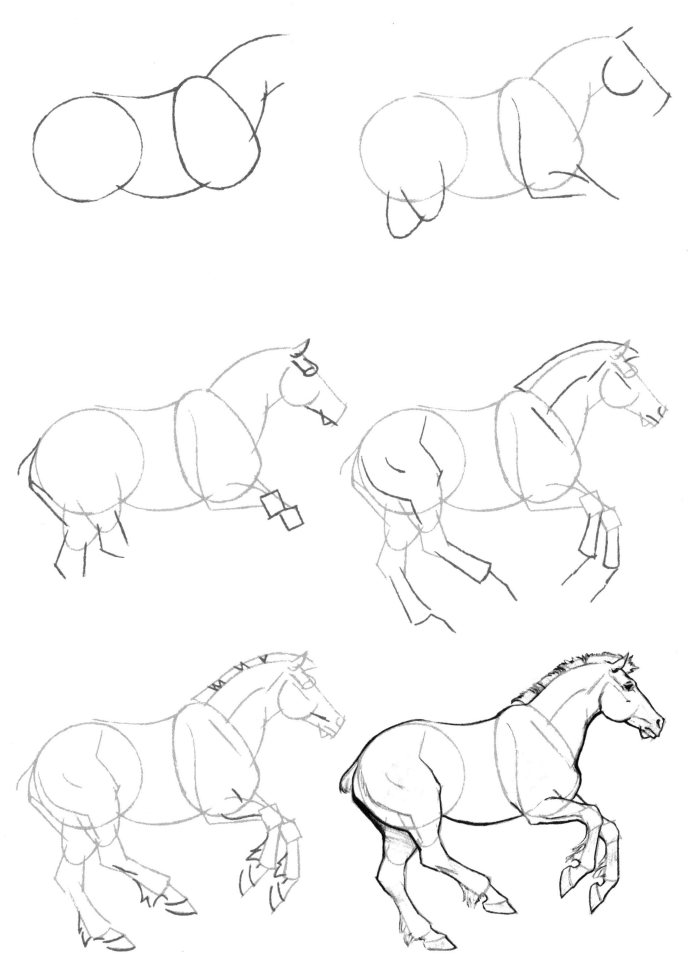

Workhorse at the canter

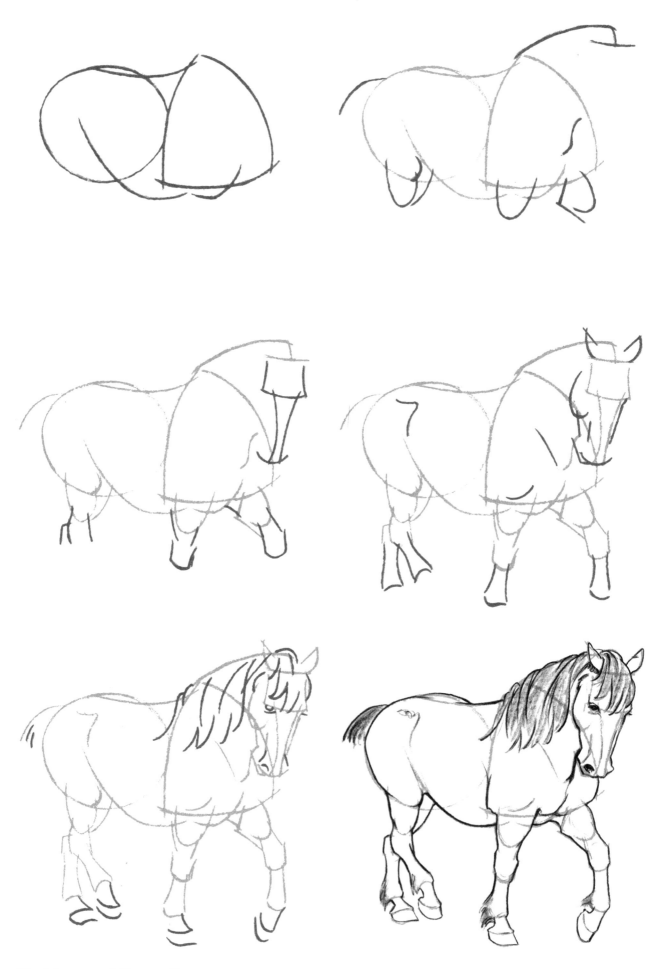

Workhorse at the walk

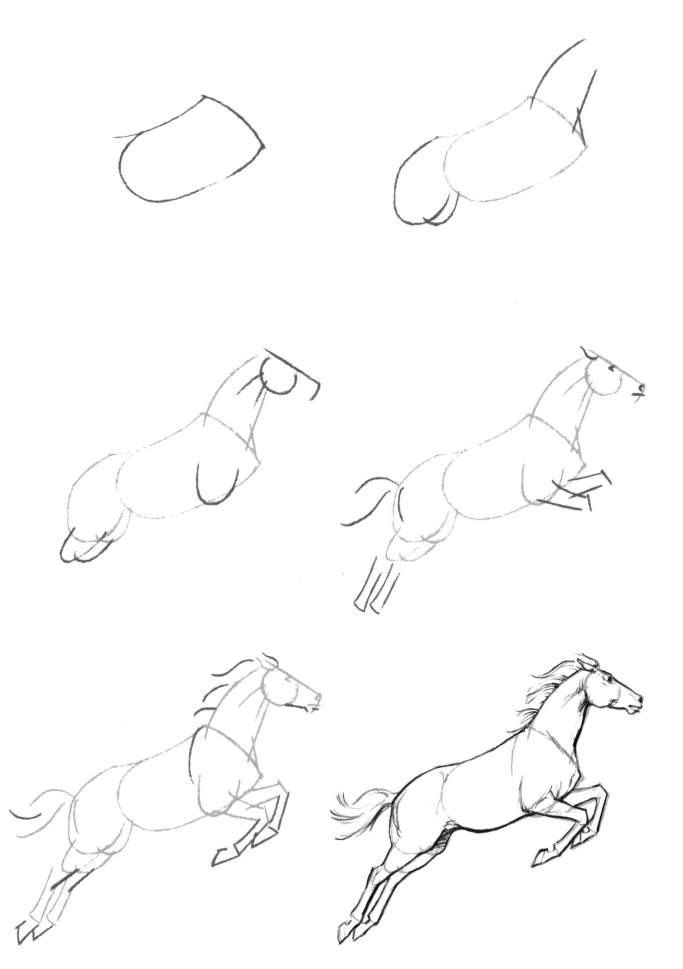

Jumping #1

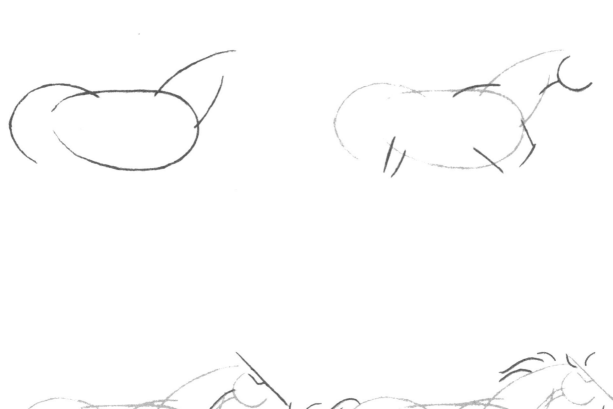

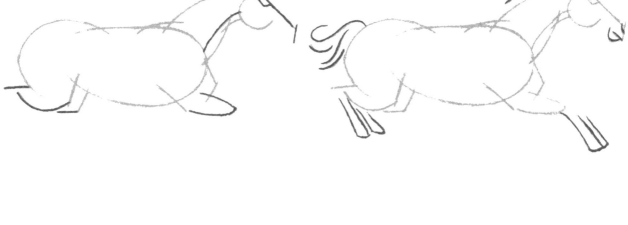

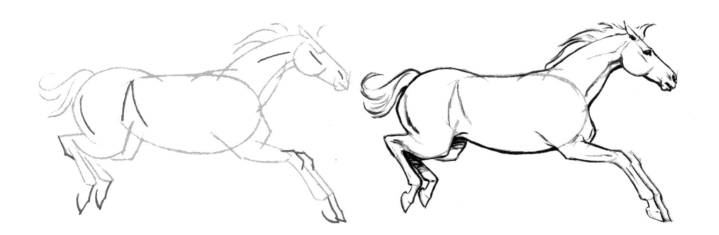

Jumping #2

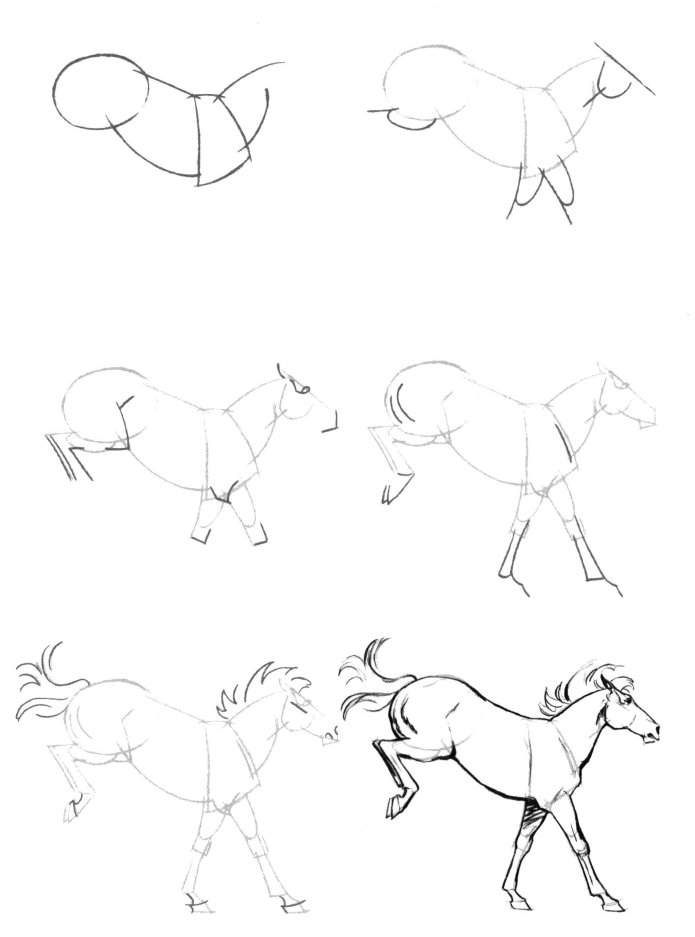

Jumping #3

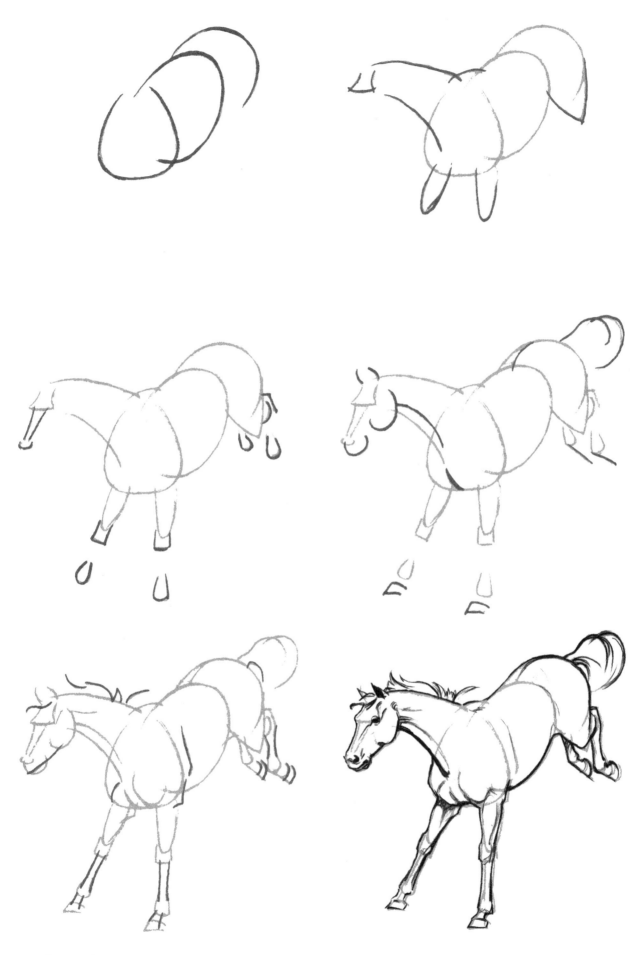

Jumping #4

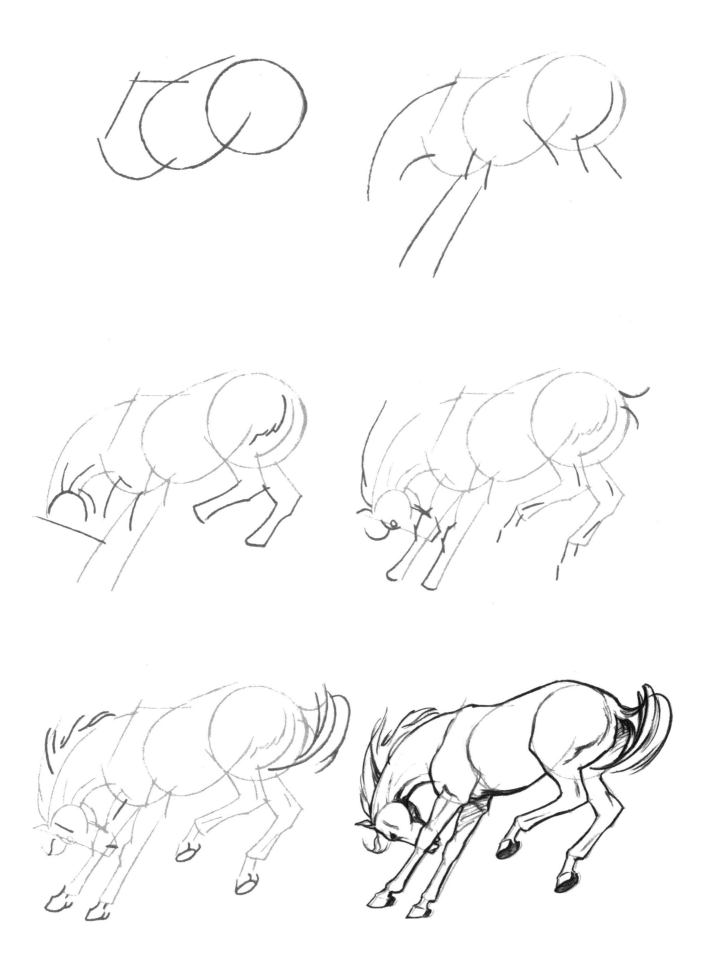

Bucking # 1

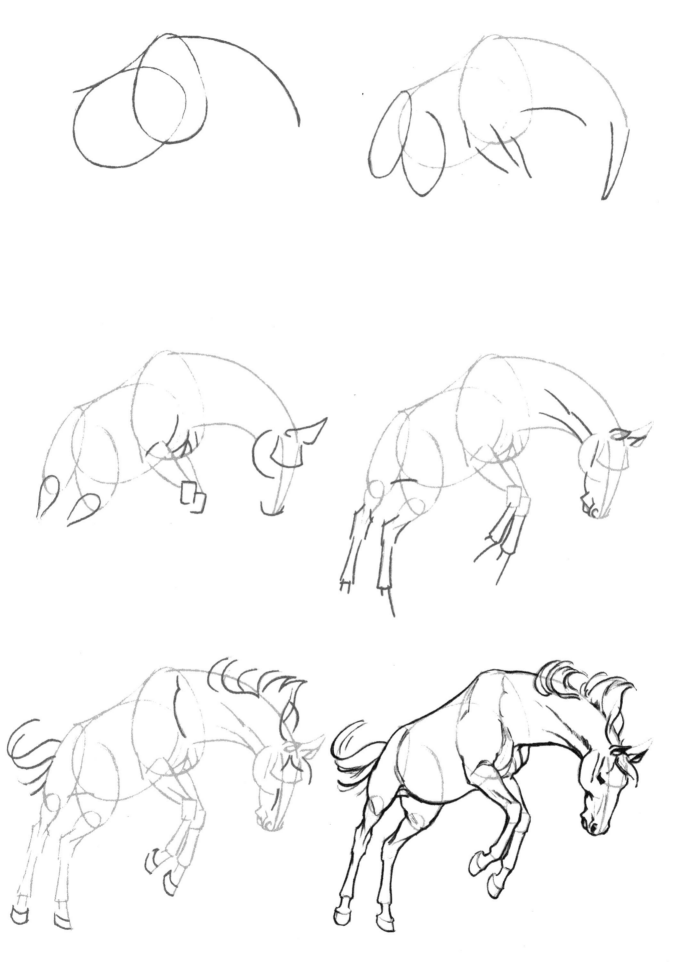

Bucking #2

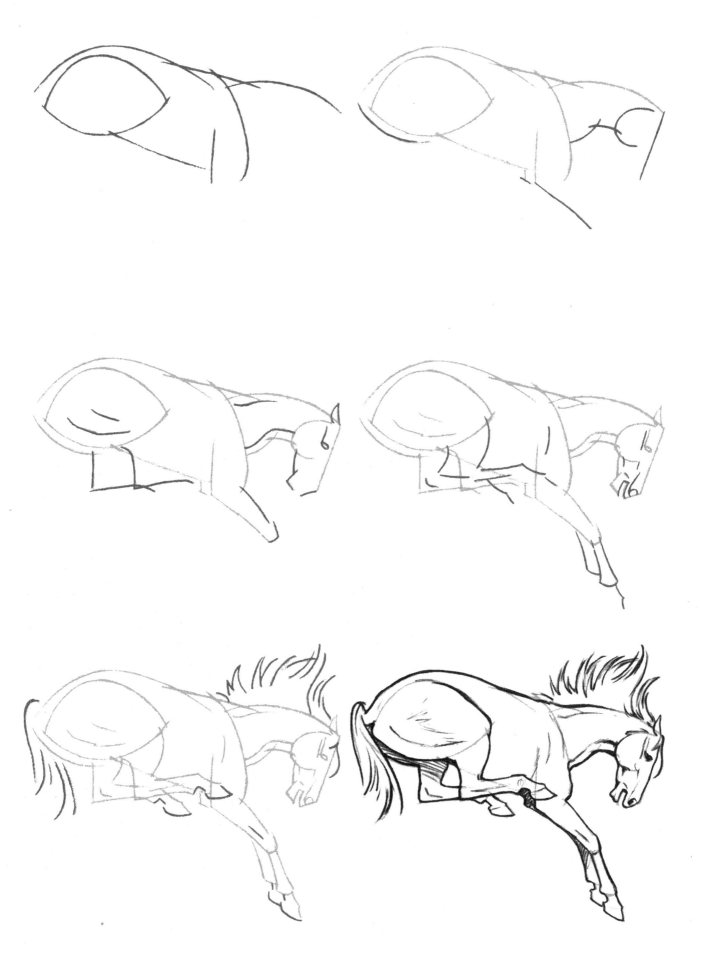

Bucking #3

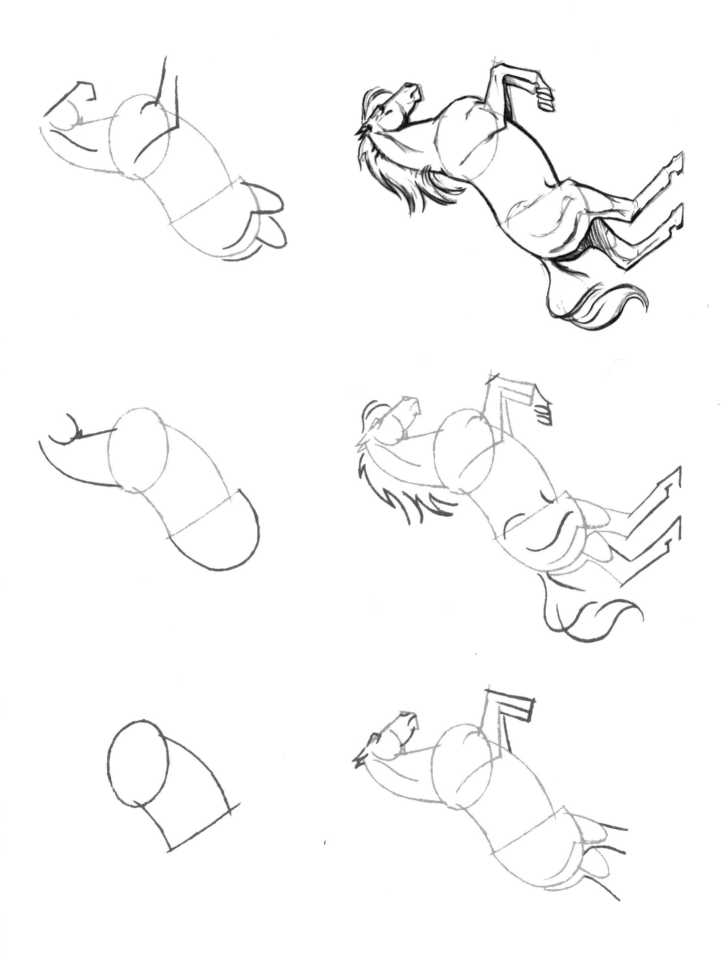

Rearing, side view

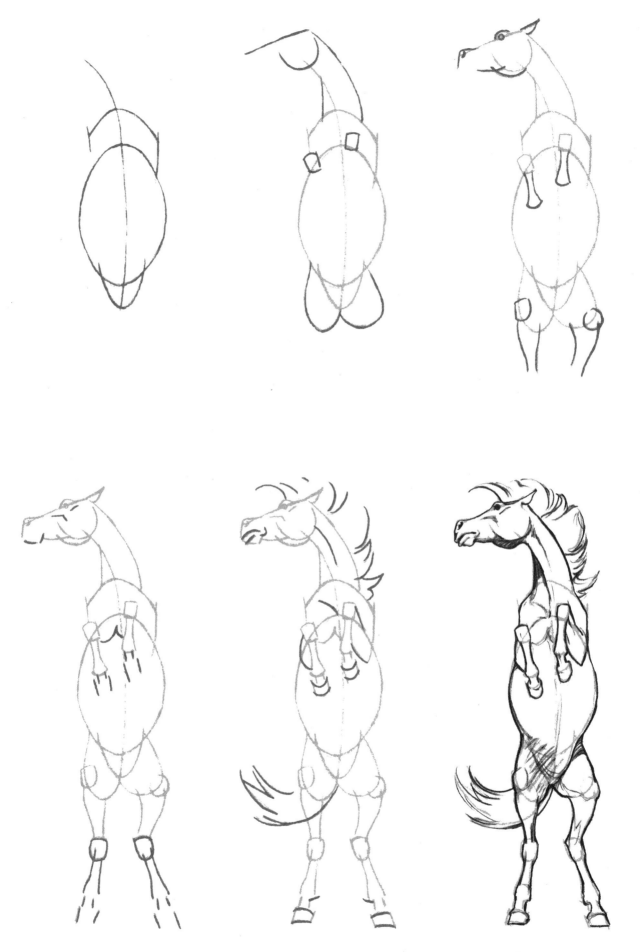

Rearing, front view

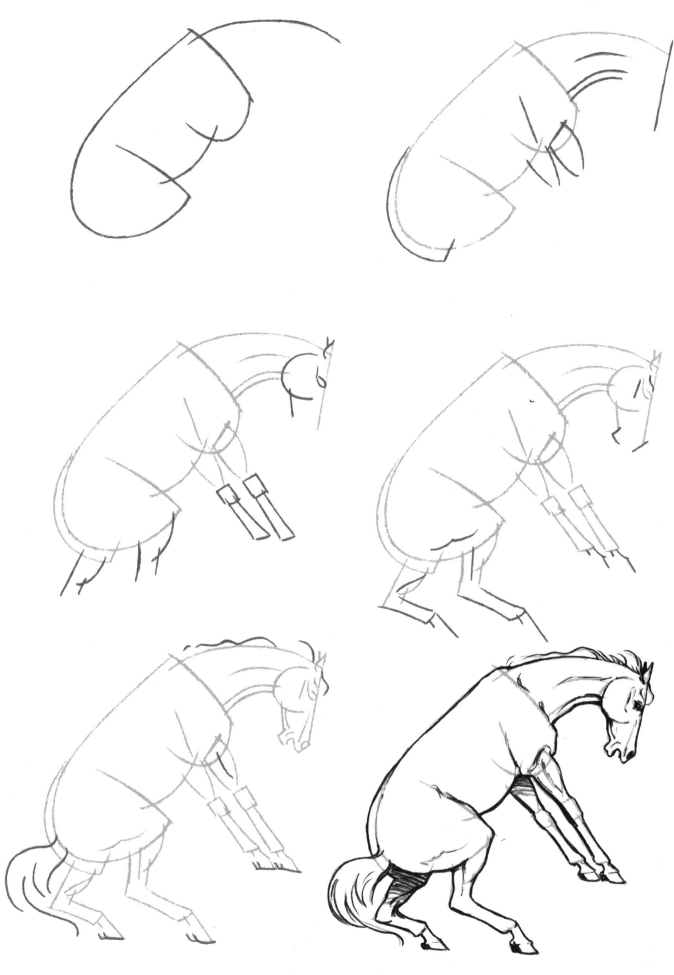

Shying

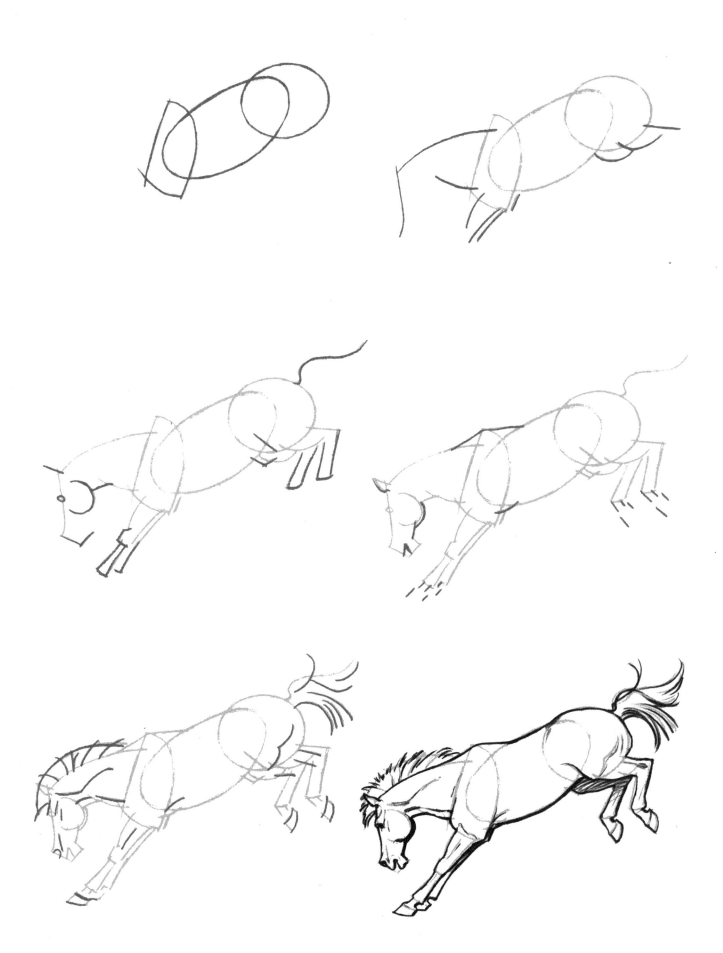

Kicking

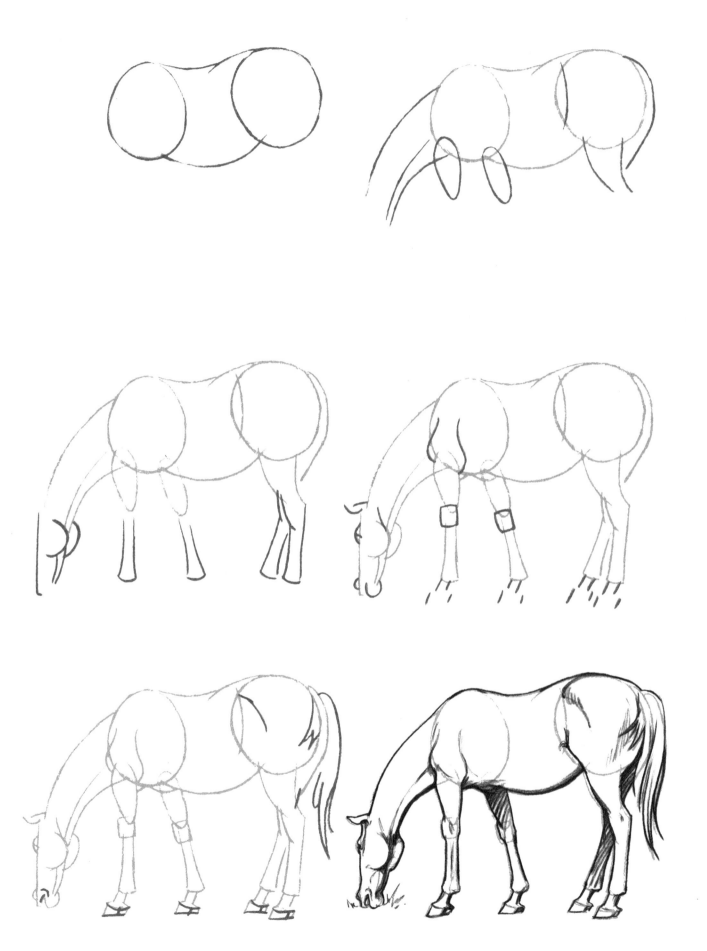

Grazing

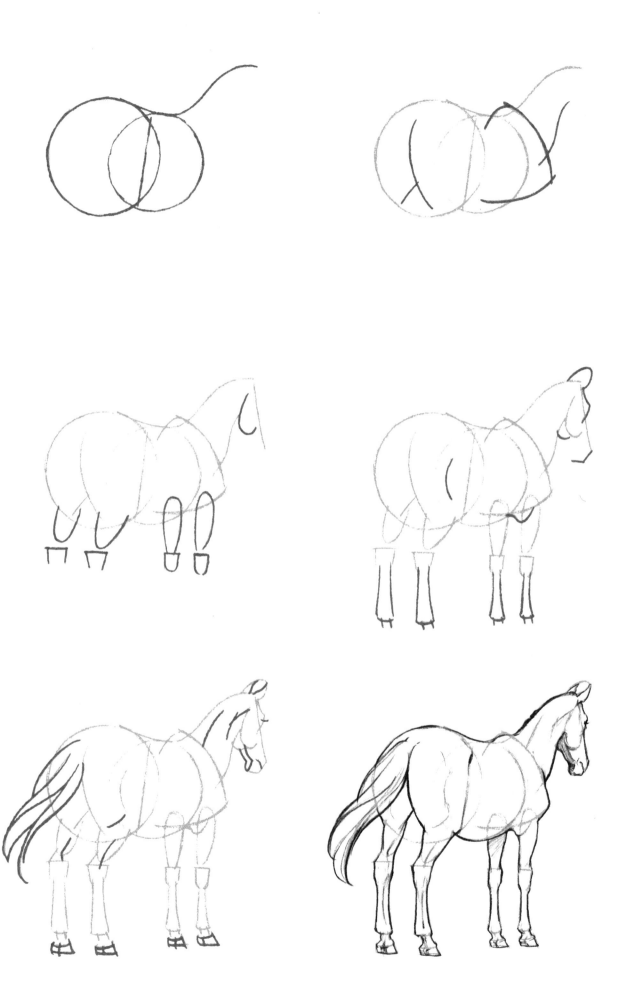

Standing, rear view

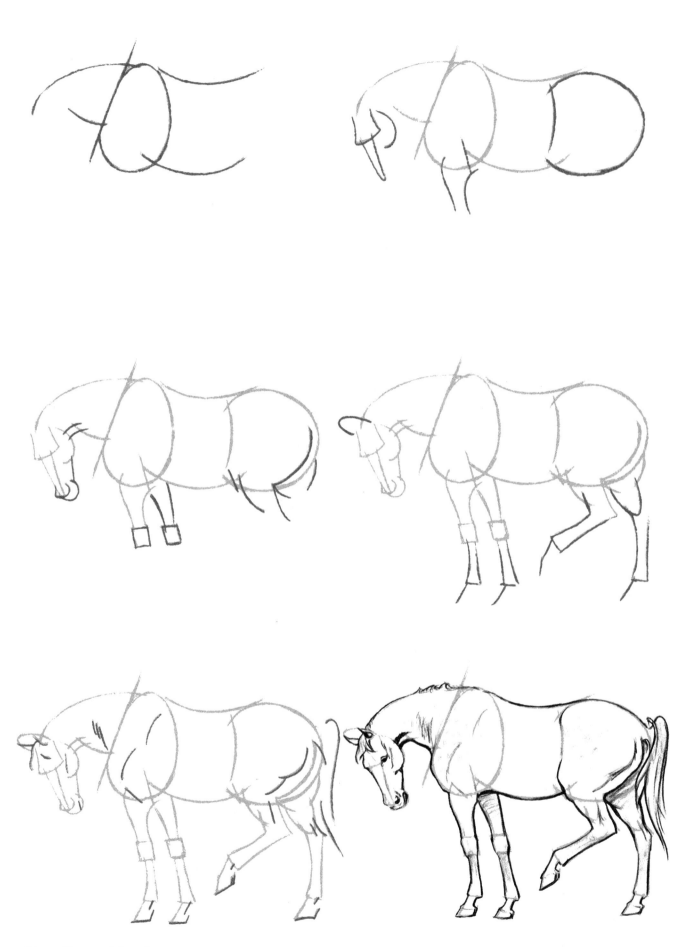

Standing, side view

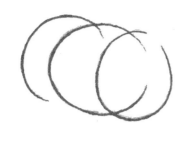

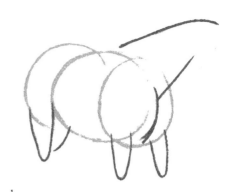

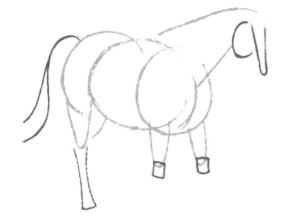

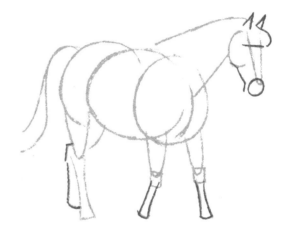

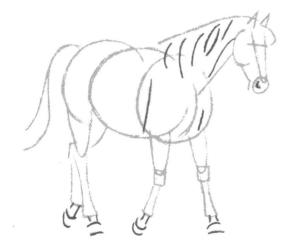

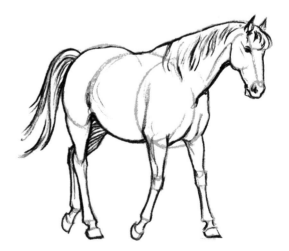

Walking, three-quarter view

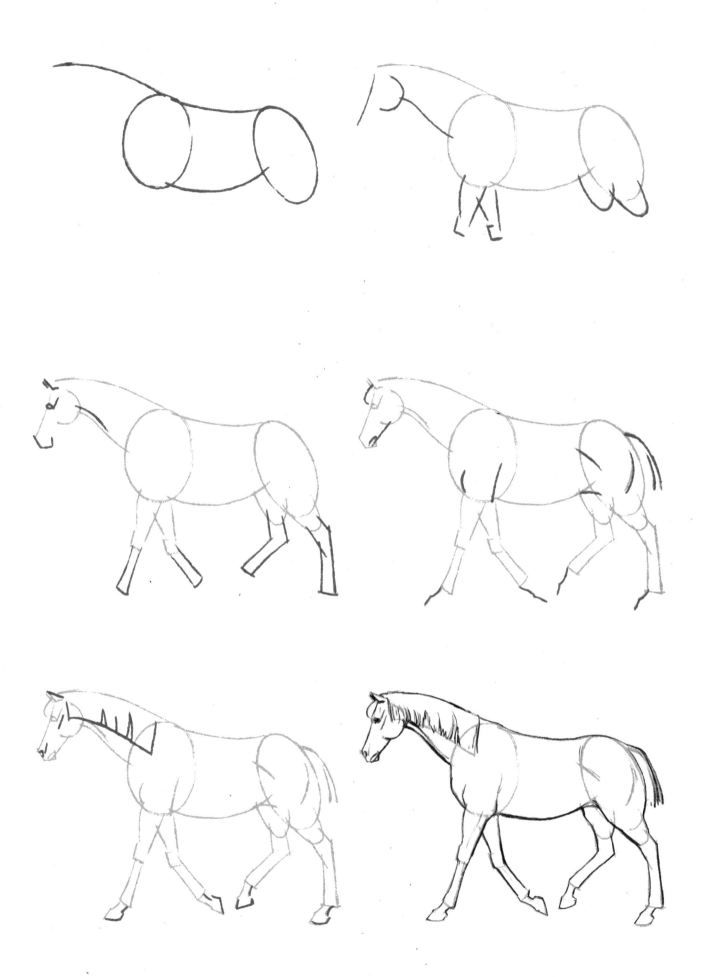

Walking, side view

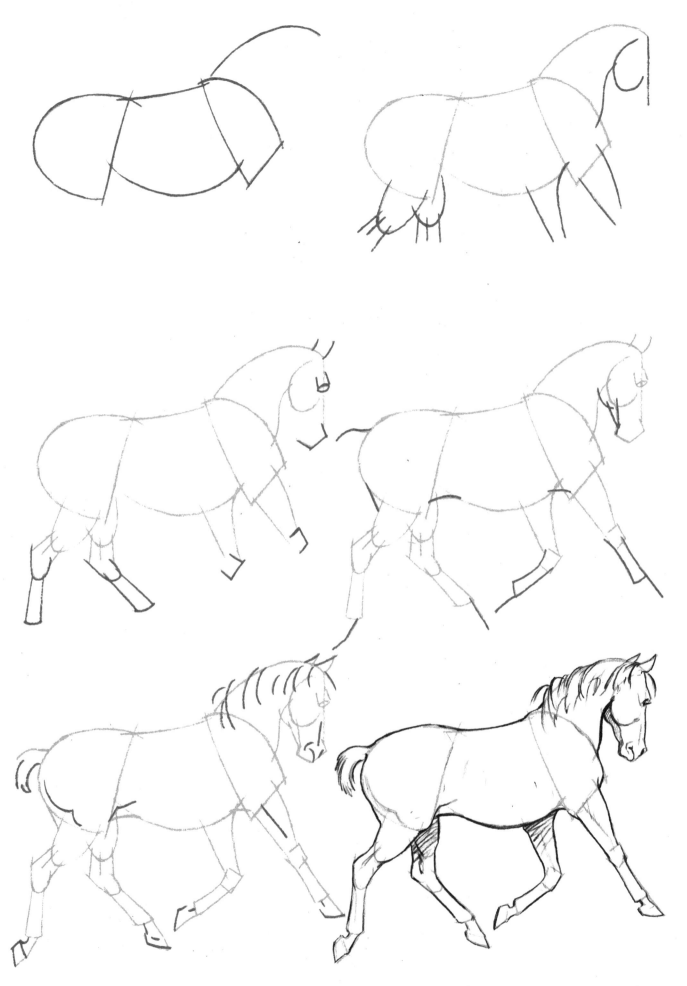

Trotting, side view

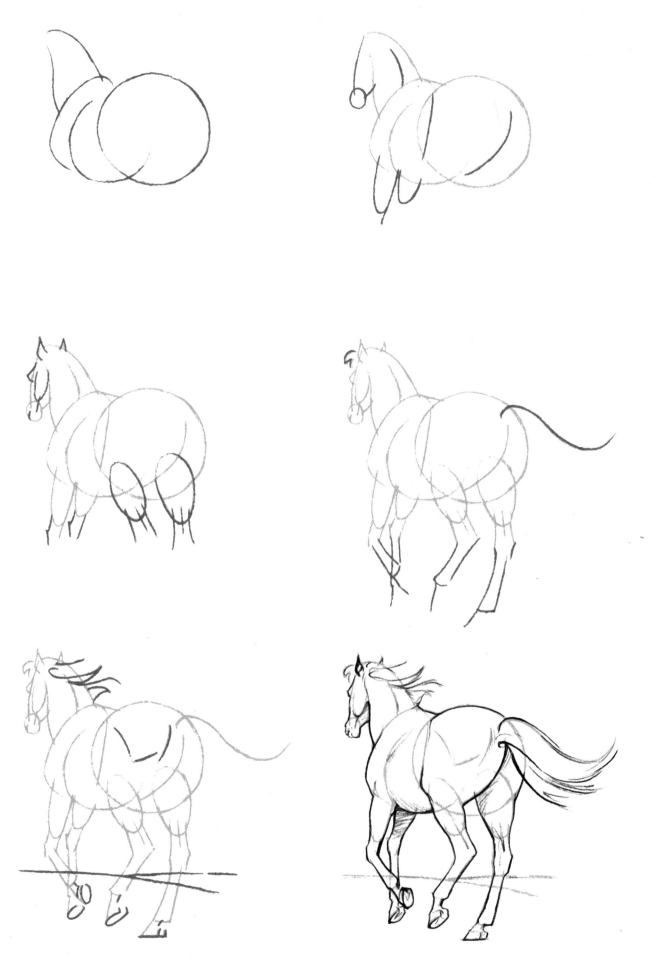

Trotting, rear view

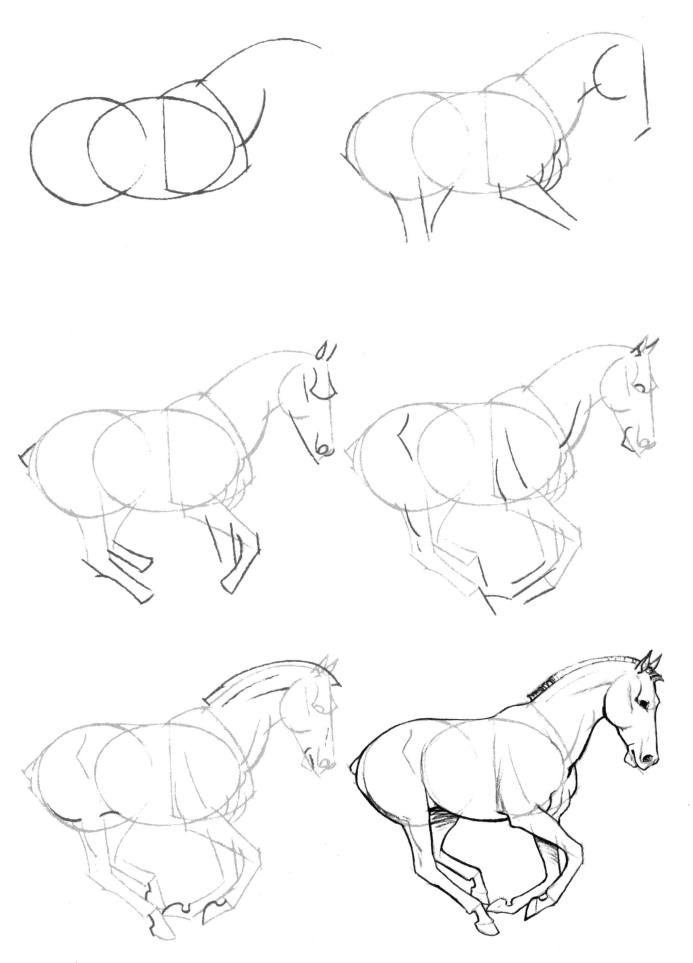

Cantering #1

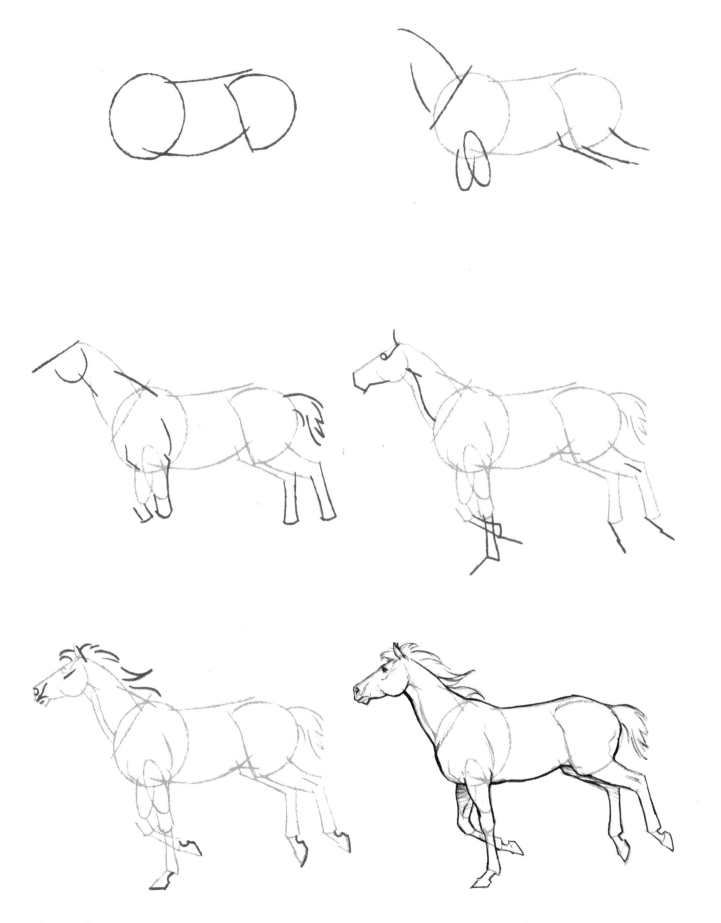

Cantering #2

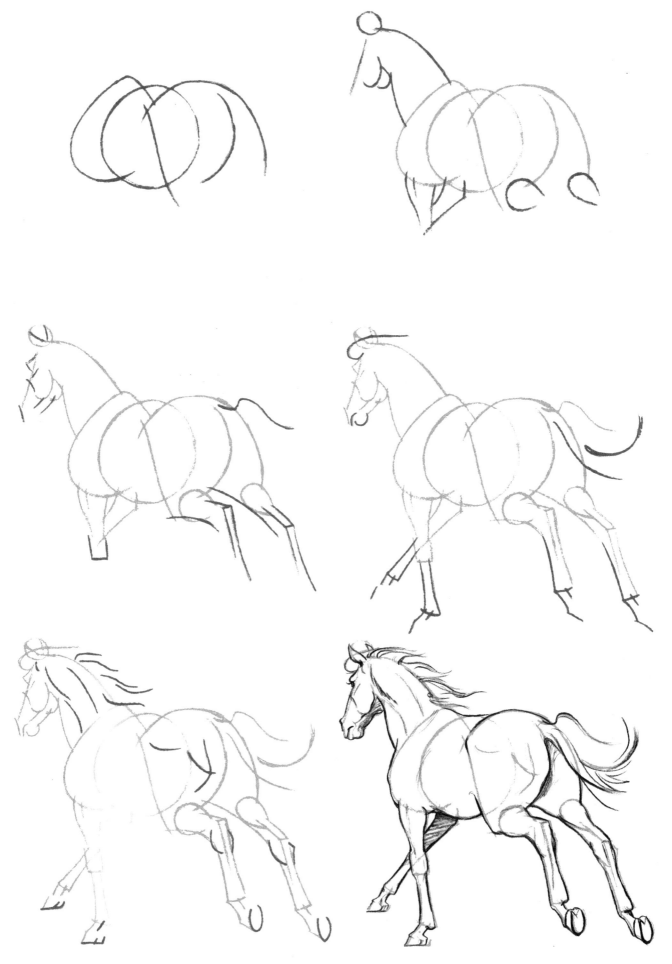

Galloping, rear view

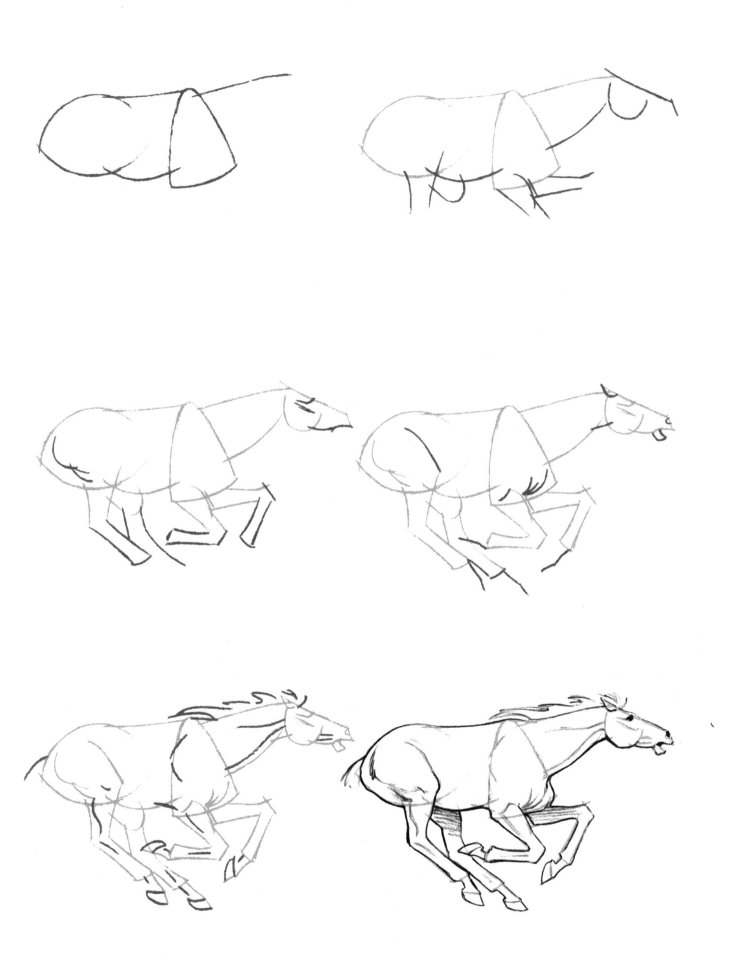

Galloping, side view

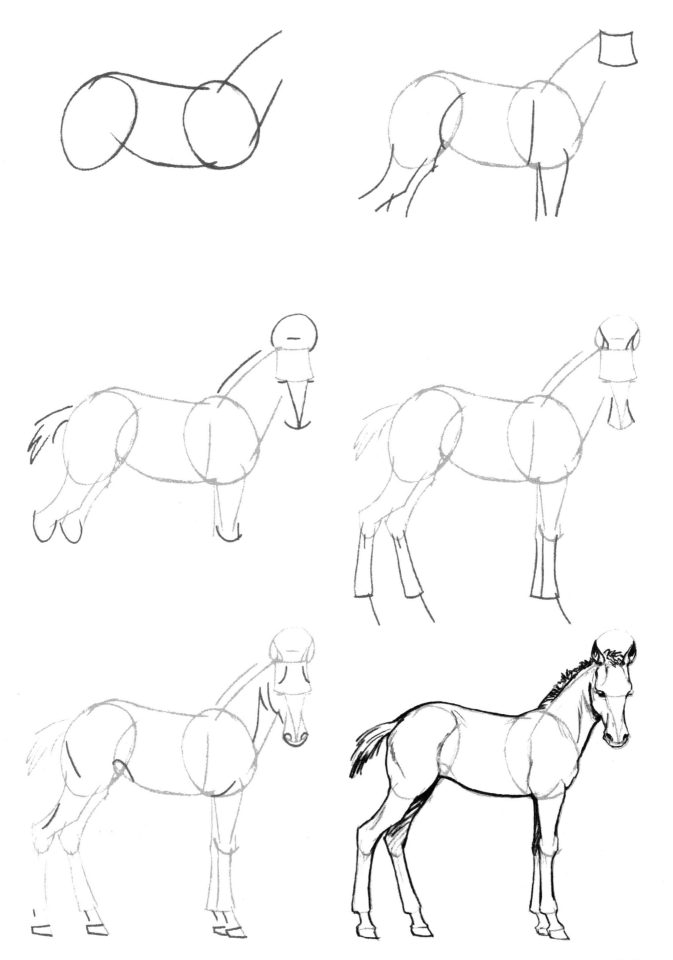

Colt

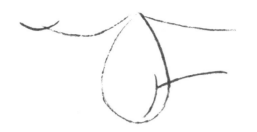
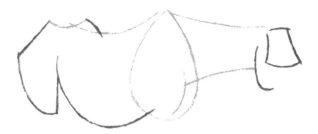
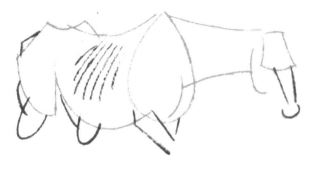
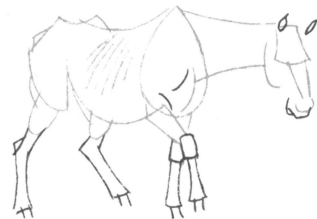
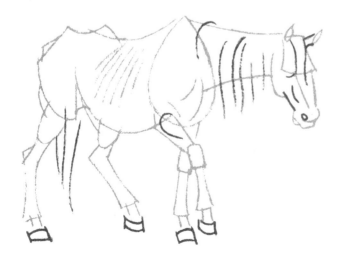
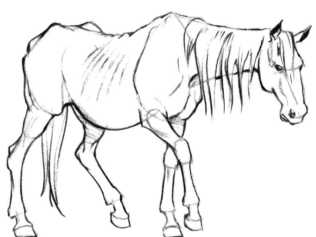

Old Age

Lee J. Ames began his career at the Walt Disney Studios, working on films that included *Fantasia* and *Pinocchio*. He taught at the School of Visual Arts in Manhattan, and at Dowling College on Long Island, New York. An avid worker, Ames directed his own advertising agency, illustrated for several magazines, and illustrated approximately 150 books that range from picture books to postgraduate texts. He resided in Dix Hills, Long Island, with his wife, Jocelyn, until his death in June 2011.

DRAW 50 HORSES

Experience All That the Draw 50 Series Has to Offer!

With this proven, step-by-step method, Lee J. Ames has taught millions how to draw everything from amphibians to automobiles. Now it's your turn! Pick up the pencil, get out some paper, and learn how to draw everything under the sun with the Draw 50 series.

Also Available:

- *Draw 50 Animal 'Toons*
- *Draw 50 Animals*
- *Draw 50 Athletes*
- *Draw 50 Baby Animals*
- *Draw 50 Cars, Trucks, and Motorcycles*
- *Draw 50 Cats*
- *Draw 50 Dinosaurs and Other Prehistoric Animals*
- *Draw 50 Dogs*
- *Draw 50 Famous Cartoons*
- *Draw 50 Flowers, Trees, and Other Plants*
- *Draw 50 Monsters*
- *Draw 50 People*
- *Draw 50 Princesses*
- *Draw 50 Sharks, Whales, and Other Sea Creatures*
- *Draw 50 Vehicles*
- *Draw the Draw 50 Way*